Narcissistic Parents

10 Tips on How to Not Hate Your Parents

Table of Contents

Introduction

Thank you and congratulations on purchasing this book, *Narcissistic Parents: 10 Tips on How to Not Hate Your Parents.* You may have one narcissistic parent, or two, or more if you have narcissistic step parents! This book is your first step in maintaining a bond with that parent, fostering the family relationship that is best for you, and moving forward into a promising future.

Having a narcissistic parent can be an incredible burden, and is a little-addressed topic in society today. Narcissism is on the rise, and the children of those who are self-absorbed are the people who suffer. Your experiences with a narcissistic parent have been difficult enough for you to seek help. This book will provide tried-and-true methods for addressing your needs in your relationship with your parent, navigating the difficult and complicated world of narcissism, and coming out safely on the other side.

It's an inescapable fact: narcissism is a real issue, and it doesn't go away. Managing a narcissistic parent involves managing an abnormal relationship. It is not normal for a parent to put themselves ahead of their children, whether their children are grown or still young and in need of care. Some parents struggle with meeting their children's needs, but strive to do so. This is not always the case with a narcissistic parent. Managing a relationship with a narcissistic parent can cause you to feel resentful. Eventually, that resent turns to hatred.

No one wants to hate their parents. It's difficult to live in a world in which you have living parents but do not have a happy, healthy relationship with them. Typically, grown children like to stay in touch with their parents and foster family bonds. It's important to involve your parents in your life, especially if you are at a stage in which you are having children of your own. Too often, children of narcissistic parents feel forced to cut their parents from their lives entirely, depriving themselves and their own children of important family bonds.

What you need to know is that it is possible to maintain a relationship with your narcissistic parent! It is also possible to eliminate your feelings of resentment and hatred. This book will provide you with ten important steps for relinquishing your hatred and resentment and moving forward with your life. You will learn how to identify a true narcissist, what narcissism means in daily life, and how to address that narcissism. You will also learn how to identify your own patterns of resentment and hatred and to address them. This book is an important tool! To best apply this advice to your own life, do not just skim the words. Take time to evaluate your own life and put it into the context of this book. Your journey toward a positive life path begins today!

Chapter One:
The Narcissist in Your Life

Before you can begin fostering a better relationship with your self-absorbed parent, it is important to understand what a true narcissist is: and whether your parent is one. The word "narcissism" comes from the Greek legend of Narcissus. Narcissus was told to be a handsome hunter, famous for his beauty. One day, he was drawn to a still pool of water in the forest, where he saw his own reflection. He became obsessed with it and would not leave, refusing to eat or drink until he died. Since the days of this legend, the term "narcissus" or "narcissism" has come to mean a person who is self-absorbed. However, there is also a very real disorder named "Narcissistic Personality Disorder." If your parent is a true narcissist, this disorder can be difficult for you to cope with.

What is Narcissistic Personality Disorder?

Narcissistic Personality Disorder is a fairly common disorder: it occurs in roughly six percent of the population, whereas disorders like Bipolar Disorder only occur in one percent of the population. Narcissistic Personality is characterized by an individual who has a grandiose sense of self-importance. They believe that they are of central importance to everyone else. They constantly need affirmation and admiration from others, and will actively seek this out. They often have little to no empathy for other human beings and will often use others as a means to achieve their own ends. For a narcissist, everything is literally about them. They are regularly arrogant, and their rudeness can be offensive to others. They are likely to feel jealous of others or feel convinced that others must be jealous of them. A narcissistic person is unable to consider another person's position or imagine themselves in another's shoes. This leads to their lack of empathy and inability to make real, strong interpersonal bonds. This can be devastating for a child.

Narcissistic Personality Disorder occurs most commonly in men, but can occur in women as well. For a person to be diagnosed as a narcissist, their symptoms and behaviors must have been present for a long period of time (at least one year). In daily life, a narcissist is likely to be condescending and easily offended by others. For example, if a busy mother trying to wrangle several children in a grocery store accidentally bumps a narcissist with her bag, the narcissist is likely to be angry and appalled at her "rudeness" without understanding the difficulty of the mother's situation. Narcissists are only concerned with how any given situation affects them personally.

The Narcissistic Parent

As a parent, a narcissist's traits become very detrimental to the child. On the outside, it can be difficult to spot a narcissistic parent. Typically, the narcissistic parent will seem to be very involved in their child's life. They will enroll their child in numerous activities. They will praise their child's accomplishments. They will seem very involved and aware of what their child is doing at all times. They will seem to be encouraging their child to be great.

Unfortunately, the narcissistic parent is not doing these things in the best interests of the child. Narcissists, who need constant admiration, seek admiration from others for their parenting skills. They see their child as an extension of themselves, and as such, are only concerned with how the child is perceived. The child must excel. The child must be a picture-perfect individual. The child is not allowed to develop their own personal identity, but is controlled by the narcissistic parent at all times. The parent is so concerned with their own needs that they will always neglect the emotional needs of the child, unless they are using the child to achieve their own means.

A narcissistic parent is controlling in many ways, but is most often controlling emotionally. A narcissistic parent sees love and affection not as something every child deserves unconditionally, but as a reward that must be earned. When a child fails to please or live up to the standards of the narcissistic parent, they may withhold love and affection as punishment. This is confusing and exhausting for the child, whether young or an adult!

Narcissistic parents will also force codependency on their children. A narcissistic parent will make it clear that fostering any other relationship means the child does not care about or deserve the parent's love. A narcissistic parent likes to keep a child close, where they can be in control. Anything that may remove the child from them—like outside relationships—must be stopped.

Children of narcissistic parents often grow up to repeat the cycle of narcissism. Because they did not have their very real psychological and emotional needs met as children, these children of narcissists become focused on their own needs as adults. Often, this translates into the same narcissistic parenting methods that the child struggled with growing up. Children may also become addicted to codependency and become unable to foster healthy relationships. They will seek out codependent relationships, often enduring abuse in the process.

Growing up under the pressure and difficulty imposed by a narcissistic parent can feel crippling. But you can break the cycle! If your parent is a true narcissist, then it is time to evaluate the methods that you can use to expel negativity and hatred from your life. Remember, this journey is about you, your future, and your children's future. Growing up under the thumb of a narcissistic parent means that you may not have ever developed independency. It can be difficult to choose to make a journey for yourself. It may feel as though you are being narcissistic, to make choices that are for your own benefit. That is not what this journey is about! This journey is about giving you back control of your life, helping you to develop independency, and, ultimately, finding a way to exist with a narcissistic parent. This journey is about removing the negative patterns from your life and pushing forward. It is time to identify the narcissist in your life and change everything!

The next few chapters will include the ten steps to changing your life and learning to let go of hatred for your narcissistic parent. Your journey is ready to begin, just turn the page.

Chapter Two:
Step One: Take a Break

It is important to have family in your life. And if you're trying to find a way to not hate your narcissistic parent, you are probably trying very hard to keep that parent in your life. But in order to develop independency and change your life, you must first take a break from your narcissistic parent. If you live at home, find a way to move out. If you've moved out but your parent calls every day, inform them that you will talk to them next week. Your break needs to be a minimum of five days' time: preferably longer. You need to take the time to clear your head and get away from the narcissist!

A narcissistic parent will always take any criticism or social difficulty personally. Be prepared, because your narcissistic parent is probably going to be angry when you give them the boot for a day or two. They may accuse you of not loving them. They may ignore you in return. Remember that this break is not permanent, and that they will likely start talking to you again when you are done with your break.

If you must explain your break to your parent, try writing out what you would like to say beforehand. Blurting out that you're reading a book on narcissism and that book says to stay away from your narcissist for a day or two is not a good idea! Be prepared with a calm, reserved statement that you are going to be taking some time to yourself.

When you do take your time to yourself, really spend time on yourself. Do not obsess over your narcissistic parent or what they will think or what they will say: this is codependency and it needs to be eradicated. Instead, spend time on some of your favorite activities. Go for a hike, or a camping trip. Treat yourself to a spa day. If it's the season, go on a good snowboarding trip. Try some new activities and really pressure yourself to get out and do things. Do not sit in front of the television for a week and do nothing! Try self-reflection with a yoga group, a meditation group, a personal journal, or some art. Get to know yourself so that you can remind yourself that you are a person who is worth loving.

This break is important because it lets you know that your narcissistic parent is not in control of you. It also lets you know that you can exist without them. Narcissistic parents spend so much time and effort controlling their offspring, it can be tough to go it alone. It's hard to find yourself when you're used to someone constantly telling you exactly who you are. But you must break your narcissist's grip on your life!

To measure the time of your break, keep it going until it isn't a chore any longer. If you have a deeply entwined relationship with your narcissistic parent, it will be very hard at first to avoid communication with them. After a while, as you start to get to know yourself and make your own decisions, the break will feel like a breath of fresh air. Once you start to feel better, more independent, you will know that the break has worked, and you will be ready to initiate contact again.

When you do initiate contact, you can expect that your parent will be angry with you. They will immediately try to draw you back into the fold of their control. Make it clear that this is not going to happen. It will be difficult, but putting your foot down now will set the precedent for the future of your relationship. If you're unsure how to do this, remember that manipulation is often subtle. But you can catch it. When your parent begins assuming that you'll do something you do not want to do (anywhere from coming to get coffee to paying for a cruise), say no. If you live with your narcissistic parent and have dinner with him/her every night, make it clear that you're going to make other plans. Make it clear that you will not be controlled. Talk about your time alone and expand on the many things you enjoyed learning about yourself. Your narcissistic parent is unlikely to be happy for you: but you are starting to pass on the message that you are no longer willing to be codependent. This is an important step for you in breaking free of the cycle of narcissistic parenting.

Chapter Three:
Step Two: Set Boundaries

The days after taking your break from your narcissistic parent are the perfect time to set some new ground rules with your narcissist. This will need to be done firmly and explicitly, or your narcissistic parent is unlikely to hear you. They will likely continue trying to manipulate you, get angry, or wait for you to get tired of trying to implement change. It is vital that you do not give in.

First, make it clear that you want your narcissistic parent in your life. Tell your parent that you care about them and want to keep them as a part of your family. Here, it will be tempting to let loose and "vent" to your parent: telling them all the things that you can't stand, telling them the many ways that they have hurt you and the many things they are doing wrong. This is not a good idea, and it is important that you refrain from doing so. A narcissistic individual will not hear and understand what you are saying to them. That is, a narcissistic individual will not understand the need to change their own behavior to suit your needs. They are only concerned with their own needs. Any emotional outburst or criticism will be taken as offensive and insulting. This will likely result in anger and emotional blackmail by the narcissistic parent, perpetuating the very cycle that you are striving to break!

Second, express the boundaries that you would like to implement. For many narcissistic parents, you may need to limit contact. For example, some narcissistic parents insist on calling their grown children frequently at work. They like to "check in." Make it clear that this behavior is unacceptable and that if they wish to "check in" during the week, they can call you in the evening, after dinner time, at home, at a reasonable hour. Make it clear that you may not always pick up the phone, and this silence does not warrant a drive across town to check on you. Perhaps your parent is overly invested in your romantic life. Nobody is every "good enough" for them. They like to scare off your significant others. Again, make it clear that this behavior is unacceptable. Defend your significant other when the situation calls for it. Do not allow your narcissistic parent to control you.

Third, make sure that you adhere to your boundaries. This can be difficult at first, especially after years of dealing with a narcissistic parent. Be patient and firm. Remind yourself of the many reasons you have to adhere to these boundaries. Separate yourself from the narcissistic parent if need be. By adhering to your new rules, you show your parent how serious you are about this situation. Giving in to their manipulation sends the message that you are still easily manipulated.

By setting clear boundaries and sticking to them, you are taking back the control of your own life. This is a key step to overcoming years of emotional control by a narcissistic parent, which is ultimately a step to ridding yourself of resentment and hatred. It is vital that you maintain your boundaries. Recognize emotional blackmail for what it is and do not give in to your parent's guilting or angry behaviors. Remain calm. Express, again, that you love them. That they are free to get in touch with you. That you would like them to be involved in your life. But that they cannot cross certain lines, because you are a grown adult.

Many narcissistic parents are skilled manipulators. When confronted with the situation of a dangerously independent child, they will often resort to extreme measures to regain control. Your parent may begin with anger, which will often feed into the "silent treatment." They may wail and accuse you of being an unloving child. When these measures fail, they may express indifference or even hatred toward you as a form of punishment. Recognize this for what it is: your parent does not hate you. Your parent suffers from a personality disorder that makes it difficult for them to accept your boundaries. Pretend you are wearing a steel suit of armor and their barbs are bouncing off.

Some narcissistic parents may see that the best manipulation solution is to "go along with it" until you forget about your boundaries or they can worm their way back into the command chair. Do not allow this to happen! Be strict and inflexible with your new boundaries. Manipulation can come from anywhere, from any seemingly tiny gesture. Do not allow your boundaries to falter.

Setting boundaries for yourself and your narcissistic parent is the first major battle in a huge war. You are taking back your life and breaking out of years of control. Before taking this step, be sure that you have had a successful "break" period as described in Chapter One. Be sure that you are ready to fight for a change in your life. Remember that this journey is for you. It is for your health. It is not selfish, it is not immoral, it is not wrong in any way. Remember that a healthy parent would approve of your pursuing happiness. Your narcissistic parent is not healthy. Your relationship with them is not healthy. It is up to you to fight the battle for a healthier, stronger life and future.

Chapter Four:
Step Three: Make Outside Friends

Narcissistic parents like to remain in control. One way of maintaining control over their children is by making sure that their children have no close bonds with anyone else. Without outside bonds, the parent forces the child to be dependent on them, leading to an unhealthy, codependent relationship. If you have found yourself in a difficult place with your narcissistic parent and are tired of being controlled, it's time to work on making friends outside of your relationship with your parent. You should seek to form meaningful, lasting bonds with others. Forming friendships will enable you to break free, be your own person, and discover what a healthy relationship looks like.

Studies show that human beings learn relationship-building skills from the example set by their parents. Children will often mimic their parents' way of forming relationships, whether they like it or not. It makes sense; if codependency and manipulation is all that you know, it's likely what you will come back to in the future. It is your comfort zone. This creates a vicious cycle of manipulation that can span for generations. The cycle can be broken! But you must be willing to put in a little effort.

By interacting with others outside of your unhealthy parental-child relationship, you are exposed to other types of bonds, likely healthy. Forming friendships will help you to build confidence. Community-building leads to confident individuals. Forming a community of friends will increase your life satisfaction. Making friends gives you a group to do activities with and a group of people to talk to about issues you may be having in your life. You are likely to find that there are many people in the world who like you for you, no strings attached. These relationships will be very important for you moving forward!

As an adult in American society, it can be difficult to make new friends. Luckily, social media has risen to the challenge with apps like Meetup.com. Find a group that participates in an activity you enjoy (Meetup has activities ranging from hiking to knitting) and get out there! You may feel awkward at first, but allow yourself to get to know others. If you aren't comfortable yet, or feel unsure, then just be a good listener for someone else. Ask questions. Get to know them. And when you're ready, tell them about yourself.

Blind online dates aren't the only way to make friends. Strike up a conversation with someone at work, and try asking them to get drinks after a long day. If you work alone (or don't like anybody that you work with), spend some free time volunteering. There is always volunteer work to be had in any given area. Find a volunteer activity that you think you'll enjoy (for example, if you like animals, then perhaps volunteer at an animal shelter). This will give you the chance to connect with others that have similar interests.

When making new friends in the community, it is important that you seek new friendships with individuals who are not well acquainted with your narcissistic parent. Remember, this life change is about you and reducing the manipulation and hatred that is present in your own life. If your parent is involved in any way with those that you reach out to, your friendship mission could be sabotaged! It is important that you form friendships away from those that can by influenced by your narcissistic parent. In order to purge the manipulation from your life, you must find some fresh friends and acquaintances.

When you have made some friends, do all that you can to foster the relationship. Make friend dates, and keep them. Listen when your friend needs a listener, and talk if you feel like sharing. If you feel safe with your friend, consider telling them about your situation with your narcissistic parent. Talking about the issue can help to get it out of your head and give you some peace. Additionally, good friends make a wonderful distraction and support system. Making good friends enables you to spend time on something other than the unhealthy relationship with your narcissist, and gives you the support system that you need. Your narcissistic parent has likely kept you isolated in an attempt to force you to be codependent. Break through that cycle by making friends with others! By relying on several people (ie, a support system) for emotional support, you will not feel the need to go back to your narcissistic parent for their love and support. Narcissistic parents use love as a bargaining chip, but that chip becomes useless when you find love and support elsewhere.

Truly spend time and effort fostering your new friendships. You are building a new life. Be honest about who you are, your likes, your dislikes, and everything in between. Find individuals who you can really connect with, and don't settle for mediocre friendships. Remind yourself that you deserve to be cared about, and find someone who is willing to provide that. Remember that friendship is a two-way street: you must be willing to reciprocate. Friendship is the lifeblood of happiness, and by fostering a good community of friends, you build a strong foundation for a happier life.

Chapter Five:
Step Four: Emotional Investment

Now that you have spent some time getting to know yourself, setting boundaries, and making friends, it's time to analyze the relationship that you have with your narcissistic parent. How do you feel about this parent? Do you love them? Hate them? Do you wish you could love them, but just can't? Do you feel frustration? Anger? Do you want explanations for their actions? Spend some time brainstorming about your feelings, and don't be afraid to delve deep into how your relationship with this parent makes you feel. Decide what it is that you want from your relationship with this parent, and be realistic. It's probably unlikely that your parent is ever going to truly invest in you. Remember, their personality disorder prevents them from truly caring more for someone else than for themselves. Everything will come back to them. It will always be them first.

Today, you reach the painful realization that your narcissistic parent cannot be changed. Their narcissism is not going to go away. Their need for control and manipulation will probably never fade. You cannot force them to repent, you cannot seek retribution, and you cannot force them to change how they feel and act. You can only change the way that you invest in the situation with this parent. This book is about making changes for yourself so that you can ultimately let go of hate and have the best possible relationship with a narcissistic parent. In this chapter, we will discuss emotional investment, and why your emotional investment in a narcissistic parent is misplaced.

This step is perhaps the most difficult step in this book. This step involves recognizing that your narcissistic parent cannot—and will never—love you unconditionally. It involves really, truly, realizing this as fact. It involves letting go of the hope that one day, your parent will love you and mean it. It involves not allowing yourself to believe your parent when they tell you they love you, that you're their favorite, or that they're proud. It involves letting go of the emotional bonds that you seek in your relationship.

This notion is a pessimistic one. When managing a narcissistic parent, it is important that you do not become emotionally invested. What this means is that you cannot place your emotional well-being in the hands of a skillful manipulator with little to no empathy for others. You must protect yourself and develop a slight barrier where your narcissistic parent is concerned. By taking your emotions out of the equation, you take away a manipulation tool that your parent currently possesses. Because they cannot toy with your emotions, you can lead the way to a healthier relationship.

Refusing to emotionally invest does not mean that you cannot love your narcissistic parent. Instead, it means that you cannot depend on their love in return. If you are constantly seeking love and affection from your narcissistic parent, you will continue to be hurt and emotionally manipulated. Fostering relationships with others will help you to find the love that you need and crave. However, you are unlikely to ever get unconditional love from your narcissistic parent, and this is always going to be a difficult pill to swallow. Everyone craves love from their parents, and it is extremely tough to be deprived of this important bond. However, your parent is a narcissist, and it's time for you to look out for yourself. Remind yourself that you are a person, who is important with or without your parent's love. By accepting that your parent is unable to love you unconditionally, and by taking emotional investment in the relationship out of the equation, you enable yourself to love your parent unconditionally. To truly love unconditionally means to love without expectation of anything in return—including reciprocated love.

When you spend time with your narcissistic parent, let go of expectations for love and affection. By constantly waiting for these cues, you set yourself up for manipulation and disappointment. Instead, enjoy laughing with your parent. Have a meal or play a board game. Avoid angering at your parent's lack of empathy for others, and maybe try quiet reminders when your parent behaves rudely. It is possible to assert your own needs without confrontation. By losing your expectations for your interaction with your narcissistic parent, you can ignore slight insults or behaviors that make you feel unloved. Remind yourself that you have love for yourself, and let that be enough. You cannot place your need for love in the hands of your parent. Releasing the need for emotional connection with your parental relationship means releasing the opportunity for resentment. Resentment is born out of the disappointment, frustration, and anger that you feel when your narcissistic parent manipulates you or lets you down. Resentment leads to hatred, an unhealthy and all-consuming feeling that will ruin your life. By adjusting your expectations, you can let go of resentment and hatred. This is a constant struggle, but one that is necessary if you want to change your life.

Chapter Six:
Step Five: Shift Your Focus

In the last chapter, we discussed the realization that your narcissistic parent is probably never going to change. This is a difficult notion to come to terms with, and you should spend time evaluating and accepting this idea. Once you feel that you have accepted it, but are ready to continue moving on, it is time to shift your focus. We've been identifying your narcissistic parent as the root of the problems with your relationship and your feelings of resentment or hatred. While it is true that your parent's narcissism is at the root of these issues, it is now time to turn your attention to yourself. In completing the rest of the steps provided by this book, and in continuing the previous steps, it is time to focus on what behaviors you engage in that facilitate resentment and hatred, and how to change those behaviors.

To begin with, you must let go of blame. Yes, your narcissistic parent has caused problems for you. Yes, they have raised you to be codependent. Yes, they have manipulated you and toyed with your emotions and made you feel insecure and unloved. Now that you have accepted that they cannot change, it is time to release the blame that you feel for them. It is time to move your focus away from how their behavior has negatively impacted your life. Assigning blame holds no benefit, and in fact leads to feelings of resentment and hatred.

Today, spend time considering how your own personality and behaviors affect your relationship with your narcissistic parent. Do you tend to set boundaries, and then fail to maintain them? Do you try to seek love from your parent, only to become disappointed, frustrated, and angry? Identify which behaviors are leading to negative patterns in your own life, and address them. Today, you are making a behavioral life change. You are accepting responsibility for your own happiness. This is an important step in seizing control of your life.

Next, it is important to identify positive behaviors and reinforce them. Do you occasionally go for a run or to the gym? Exercise is an excellent way to spend time alone with your thoughts while increasing your overall physical and mental health. Try to encourage fitness in your life, and spend time focusing on activities that you enjoy. Do you like to read? Buy some new books or get a library card and read something new this week. Spend time reinforcing the positive behaviors that are already present in your own life.

By reinforcing positive patterns, rather than negative ones, you will find yourself shifting away from the anger and resentment that has stemmed from your relationship with your parent. By letting go of blame, and by eliminating negative behaviors, you can slowly begin to replace negative patterns with positive ones. Shifting your focus away from hatred and resentment gives you time to care about other things. Over time, that hatred and resentment diminishes until you find that you no longer need it as a buffer for the scars of dealing with a narcissistic parent. Resentment and hatred are characterized by intrusive, repetitive thought processes that will dominate your life if you choose to feed into them. Releasing hatred and resentment will take time and significant effort. Focusing on other positive things will help you to replace these patterns with healthier means of emotional support.

Focusing on other relationships, as discussed in Chapter Four, is another way to inject positivity into your life. You may also consider getting a pet or starting a garden. Find something living to connect to that creates feelings of positivity in your life. Investing in something new and meaningful will give you hope. Nothing demolishes hatred and resentment like hope does.

As you move forward, continue replacing negative patterns with positive ones. Be honest with yourself. When you identify a negative pattern, do not feel ashamed—there is no need for guilt. Simply identify the pattern as negative and strive to replace it in the future. Every day is another opportunity for change. Mistakes will always happen. There will be days that you feel sad, days that you feel angry, and, yes, days that you burn with hatred. But by replacing these days with positive actions, little by little, you will form a life that is built on the positive patterns. Remind yourself that life is a journey, and nothing happens overnight. You are striving to break free of years of conditioning. It is a difficult and often frustrating path. By focusing on yourself, your needs, and positive changes, you can make a significant difference.

Chapter Seven:
Step Six: Invest in Yourself

Now that you have shifted your focus from changing your narcissistic parent's behavior, it is time to invest in yourself. You have started to identify negative patterns and you are replacing them with positive ones. This is an excellent time to continue the journal that you may have started in Chapter Two. Keep a log of your progress and your difficulties. Every so often, glance back through the pages to note how far you have come! This is a great way to keep yourself encouraged and on task.

You have been working to let go of blame, resentment, hatred, and seeking your parent's love. You have taken the major steps in freeing yourself from your narcissistic parent's manipulation! Now, it is truly time to invest in yourself. This does not mean becoming as narcissistic as your parent is. You should not seek your needs over the needs of others in your life. For example, fostering friendships benefits you in that you have a friend, but you should seek to care for the needs of your friends selflessly. Do not begin using others as a means to replace your parent's lack of love: instead, seek to replace the need for that love from within. You are a complete person, and spending time for yourself is a way to train yourself to let go of codependency.

By investing in yourself, you are learning to love and care for yourself. Make health changes, and consciously seek to build a healthy body with good food and exercise. Improve your social health by fostering your friendships. Take control of your home life by redecorating, cooking yourself a nice meal, or adopting an animal as a pet. Spend time on your education and on learning. If you have the means, take some time to travel. Find what makes you feel good and pursue it.

You are free from the manipulation of your narcissistic parent. Now is the time to consider what kind of person you want to be and what future you want to pursue. Whether this means pursuing a new career or taking some time for spiritual healing is all up to you! Narcissistic parents typically inhibit the development of their child's personality in their need to make their child codependent. Often, activities that the child competes in, classes the child works hard in, and colleges that the child chooses are determined by the narcissistic parent. Investing in yourself now will not completely reverse the effects of this upbringing, but it can help you to lead a happier, fuller life in the future. You have worked to let go of the past: now is time to plan the rest of your life.

If you haven't already, you may consider seeing a therapist, counselor, or going to a support group as you continue to invest time in yourself and your healing process. Letting go is an extensive process that can take years, and it can be incredibly difficult to learn to spend time on yourself without becoming a narcissist like your parent. A counselor or support group can give you vital, professional support as you navigate this difficult path. You can learn how to look out for yourself while still staying attuned to the needs of others. You can learn how to forge a new path without relying on the codependent relationship that you had with your narcissistic parent.

Counseling and support groups often have a stigma attached to them, which is unfortunate, as they are a valuable resource. There is no shame in seeking help for your life! These venues can have several unexpected benefits. Besides providing support as you go through these changes in your life, you will connect with others, gain some listening ears, and perhaps form a circle of friends. You can work through your feelings of resentment, anger, and hatred as they come. If you are uncomfortable with the notion of therapy sessions or support groups, there are many online, anonymous groups and therapists that can be reached for assistance.

As you walk the path to your future, know that this journey is your life. People, including friends and family, will always come and go, but the one person you always need to live with is you. Investing in this person and their health, getting to know them, providing them with spiritual or emotional support, and taking time for them, is a huge step in building a happy, stable life. By learning to consider your own needs and by pursuing the things that make you happy, you are taking the reins and asserting yourself. Eventually, the resentment toward your narcissistic parent will be irrelevant, and the hatred will begin to melt away. As you become enough for yourself, there will no longer be a need to hate your parent. Focus on yourself, and let the rest of it go.

Chapter Eight:
Step Seven: Build Self-Confidence

You are well on your way to officially leaving behind hatred, narcissism, and all the difficulties of a narcissistic parent! Now that you have spent time on yourself, mapped out your goals and ideas, and perhaps even considered therapy or support groups, it's time to build your confidence. Often, it's easy to see the life that you want, and to know how to get there, but actually doing it is another matter entirely. It's easy to say that you'll go to the gym every other day, but when you're picking up those 10 lb weights next to a Hulk lifting 100 lbs per arm, your confidence may whither. Accomplishing your goals and reaching your dreams is all about confidence!

For those that have spent time under the thumb of a narcissistic parent, self-confidence may be an elusive entity. Narcissistic parents are known for decreasing their child's self-confidence in order to maintain that child's dependency on the parent. Narcissistic parents will often take credit for a child's accomplishments—as in, "Oh she's good at soccer, she gets it from me, of course, I was a champion at her age and she isn't..."—and redirecting attention from their child to themselves. This can be hugely devastating to a child's sense of self-worth and self-confidence. These traits often develop in early childhood, and if never developed, can remain a problem that can plague a person for a lifetime.

Building self-confidence doesn't have to be a horribly difficult feat. Take some time and think about what makes you feel proud or good about yourself. Do you have an awesome pair of jeans? Did you get a perfect score on a paper? Can you fix a car with your eyes closed? Just as in Chapter Seven, you should seek to reinforce behaviors with positive outcomes. If an activity makes you feel confident, do it! If an outfit makes you feel confident, wear it! Identify the things that make you confident and bring them to the forefront of your life.

Of course, there will always be those inescapable moments that leave you feeling weak and depressed. There will be days that you feel fat, or stupid, or alone. What do you do then?

At these times, you should seek positive reinforcers. One example would be positive self-talk. Remind yourself of the things you have to be proud of. Remember something that you have accomplished. Avoid engaging in negative behaviors to make yourself feel better: you should not, for example, "eat your feelings," nor should you ever put down another person to make yourself feel better. If you need to clear your head, go for a walk. The outdoors and the fresh air are a great way to clear your head and distract you from pervasive negative thoughts.

If you are having extreme issues with self-confidence, therapy or support groups are again a good idea. You can also invest time in strategies to help you when you are feeling badly. You can carry objects with you in your wallet or purse that bring a smile to your face—a silly photo or a worry stone, for example. Download music onto your smartphone and take headphones with you—listening to music can help to provide you with an "escape." Talking to someone is always a wonderful idea.

Your self-confidence should always come from within. Seeking affirmation from others, or taking confidence by minimizing others is not true self-confidence. As you build your self-awareness, self-confidence will come! Narcissistic parents often ensure that their child's self-confidence only comes from expressions of approval by the parent. This ensures that the child is dependent on the parent and easy to manipulate. By building your own self-confidence, you are breaking this cycle and allowing yourself to be your own person.

Remember that building confidence is a process. It takes practice! The old saying "fake it till you make it" is absolutely true. Pretend that you are invincible until you actually are. The day will come that you will find that you are not pretending anymore. You aren't pretending that mean words don't hurt, and you aren't pretending not to care about your parent's attempts at manipulation. Instead, you are a strong, confident individual who doesn't need to give in to others. You can do this!

Chapter Nine:
Step Eight: Self-Recognition

On your journey to finding yourself and building confidence, you may find that it is difficult to give praise to yourself or to feel very proud of your achievements. Why is this? As discussed in Chapter Eight, narcissistic parents often take credit for their child's accomplishments. A narcissistic parent craves attention and praise from others, so they will push their children to accomplish more. An accomplished child reflects well on that child's parents in today's Western societies, so the narcissistic parent is glad to step up and take the credit for what the child worked hard to accomplish. The child is briefly rewarded with the parent's approval, affection, and expressions of love, but is denied the recognition they deserve for working hard and reaching a goal. The goal was never theirs—their parent always took ownership of it.

This appropriation by narcissistic parents can have lasting damage on an individual. It can lead to an individual who has difficulty taking pride in their achievements, or it can lead to an individual who aggressively seeks praise for their achievements. Children who have been conditioned to accept their parent's ownership of their work may have difficulty taking pride in their accomplishments. Children whose parents both took ownership and praised them in reward for their accomplishments may become aggressive praise-seekers. Because their emotional needs were not fulfilled as children, these individuals seek emotional fulfillment as adults in a way that they were deprived of.

As an adult who is breaking the cycle of narcissistic parenting, it is important for you to take ownership of your accomplishments. The feelings of resentment and hatred that you may have experienced toward your narcissistic parent may come from a lifetime of giving up your self-recognition. If you have accomplished something, it is okay to acknowledge it! Congratulations! Do not sell yourself short when you have worked hard and achieved.

Likewise, you should be sure that you are giving yourself the recognition you deserve without aggressively seeking it from others. Shouting about your accomplishments to garner attention and praise is not healthy and should not be pursued. If you feel the need to get the praise of others for your good deeds, consider why this is. Why do you need praise to feel validated?

Self-validation is the result and lifetime benefit of engaging in self-recognition. When you can objectively determine that you have accomplished something that is valuable to yourself in one way your another, you are gaining self-validation. You are acknowledging that you are a person of worth who contributes good things to the world. You do not need the praise of others to accomplish this! This book is all about building independence, breaking free of the cycle of narcissism, and letting go of hatred. Self-validation enables you to do all of these things.

As you examine your accomplishments and actions, try to reach a place in which you can be critical of yourself in a positive way. For example, perhaps you could have gone to the gym today, but chose to remain on the couch all afternoon instead. Instead of allowing your self-confidence to plummet, instead of seeking validation from others, critically assess the situation. Yes, you missed the gym. Yes, you should have gone. You will go tomorrow! Perhaps, at the end of the month, you have met your goal for weight loss. Congratulations! You should feel able to congratulate yourself and engage in self-recognition in a positive, constructive way.

As you take back your life, taking ownership of your accomplishments will have applications for every facet of life, not just your relationship with your narcissistic parent. Having the confidence to recognize your own worth, validation, and accomplishment is a valuable tool in today's world. You will become a strong individual who cannot be pushed around. It is time to recognize your own power and live it!

Chapter Ten:
Step Nine: Love, Not Dependency

You have embarked on a wonderful journey of self-reflection, self-improvement, and self-validation. Most of this book is geared toward the many things that you can do to change your own life. Your interactions with your narcissistic parent had instilled in you feelings of frustration, anger, or hatred, but this book shifted your focus inward, on everything that you can do to let go of these feelings and increase your own happiness. You may have formed friends, joined a support group or a gym, or maybe you've been spending a lot of time with yourself and your journal. Maybe you were in a relationship before reading this book, and maybe not. Maybe you're looking to start a new relationship. Eventually, most of you will probably be engaged in a relationship with a significant other. This chapter is about navigating the path of those kinds of relationships, how having a narcissistic parent affects your relationship bonds, and how to break the cycle.

As discussed throughout the book, narcissistic parents will almost always force codependency on their children, whether consciously or subconsciously. A narcissist desires to be the center of the child's world, and cannot allow other relationships to thrive which might take away from the child's dependency on the narcissist. This teaches the child that relationships should be centered around dependency. Studies show that the children of narcissists will often seek codependent relationships, often enduring abuse in the process.

A codependent relationship is characterized by sacrificing your own needs for the benefit of your partner. Initially, this can feel like a healthy and necessary part of a relationship.

However, you may eventually realize that your partner is an emotional vampire—that is, feeding off of your emotional support without providing any in return. Codependency involves a lack of self-sufficiency on your part, otherwise known as "clinginess." You make significant sacrifices for your partner's needs without getting anything in return. If you cannot find or imagine life satisfaction without a particular person, you are likely engaged in a codependent relationship.

Children of narcissists often confuse dependency with love. Unconditional love is the notion that you love someone for who they are, without any conditions or strings attached. Unfortunately, sacrificing your own needs can be confused with unconditional love. This is an unhealthy negative pattern. Remember that unconditional love is not the same as unconditional sacrifice. You deserve to be loved in return, and if you are not, it's time to leave.

If you have spent time seeking self-fulfillment, then you are ready to take the reins in your love life. Just as you can let go of your narcissistic parent's influence, so too can you let go of the person in your relationship if it is unhealthy. Remember that you are enough on your own.

As you form new relationships or change current ones, focus on loving the other person while maintaining your own standards and boundaries. Nobody has the right to expect you to make unlimited sacrifices for their happiness or continued love. Be gentle but firm in your boundaries. Remind this person that a refusal to give in does not indicate a lack of love.

As you form relationships, continue to take time to yourself. It is easy to become overly involved in a relationship and to quickly become codependent. This can be avoided if you continue to be a little bit "selfish" each week by taking time alone to do things that you enjoy, alone or with friends. Do not allow your relationship to become the only important thing in your life. Remind yourself that you and your needs are important.

As you break down the walls of codependency, you further destroy the influence your narcissistic parent has had on your life. As you learn to love unconditionally without becoming codependent, you can even begin to reform a relationship with your narcissistic parent based on your refusal to become codependent. By changing the terms of the relationship, you are no longer vulnerable to the manipulation and damage that the relationship has caused you in the past. You can engage in a fulfilling familial interaction without becoming beholden to that parent. However, you do not have to reform a relationship with this parent. You can continue practicing love without codependency in other contexts. Without codependency, you will be a stronger and happier individual.

Chapter Eleven:
Step Ten: Break the Cycle

You are nearing the end of your journey. You have broken the grip of your narcissistic parent on your life. You have delved into yourself and discovered who you are and what you want. You have replaced negative patterns with positive ones. You have started to let go of the past, relinquish your grip on anger and hatred, and look to the future. You have fought against codependency and engaged in self-validation. Now, it is time to end the cycle of narcissism once and for all.

An unfortunate fact is that narcissistic children will often grow up to become narcissistic parents. Because they were emotionally abused and manipulated as children, the children of a narcissist have gaping holes in their emotional development. As adults, they often become narcissists themselves, with little empathy for others, entirely focused on filling these emotional holes. As parents, they wind up repeating the same cycles that their parent did, because it is all that they know. The cycle continues generation after generation. It seems hopeless, but you can stop it.

To begin with, spend time on selfless activities. It is likely that you have some emotional needs that were unmet by your narcissistic parent, or you would not be reading this book. As you move forward, find some volunteer work. Get involved. Spend ample amounts of time caring for other people. Put yourself in their shoes, and actively practice empathy. In this way, you reinforce your empathetic tendencies, instead of allowing them to die off as you seek your own emotional fulfillment. As you keep busy helping others, you will find that you are becoming emotionally fulfilled anyway. Positive social interaction is good for the soul. Helping others gives you some perspective, and helps you to heal.

If you have children or are planning to have children, remember how you were raised. Remember all the manipulation, the frustration, and everything that led you to purchasing this book. As you move forward, resolve that this is not going to happen in the next generation. Allowing the cycle to continue means that it is still present. It means that you have not moved on. You are still harboring feelings of anger and hatred. Breaking the cycle with your own children is yet another way to let go.

If you are unsure how to manage raising your child(ren) without repeating the tendencies of your narcissistic parent, attend a parenting class. Invest time in reading literature on raising your child. And actively recognize that your child is not an extension of yourself. They are their own person, just as you have striven to be throughout this book.

Your child has ownership of their accomplishments. Be proud of them! But do not be proud *for* them. Allow your child to pursue their own interests and set their own goals, rather than forcing image-based ideas into their lives. Give up the notion that others are judging you based on your children's accomplishments—it is unimportant in the face of their happiness and development. Put your children's safety and happiness above your own needs. Never withhold love as a form of punishment. Remind your children that you love them unconditionally.

Raising a child in this way will give you such fulfillment as you have never felt before. Being a truly selfless parent will be such a different relationship from the relationship that you had that it will be fulfilling in and of itself. Breaking the cycle of narcissism will enable you to form a lasting, healthy family bond with your own child.

As your child grows, avoid behaviors that encourage codependency. Encourage your child to be independent, to explore, and to engage in activities for themselves. Allow your child to make decisions. Allow your child to grow up and leave you. This is healthy, and it is right. Holding on to your child or forcing them to be codependent is putting your needs above the child's and Is a trait of narcissism.

By raising your child differently, outside of the pattern of narcissism, you have truly banished the effects of your narcissistic parent from your life. You have broken the cycle! Raising a child in a healthy way will pave the way for generations of future healthy children and healthy relationships. This is something to be proud of, and something to draw fulfillment from.

You may not be someone who has children or ever intends to have children. You can still break the cycle of narcissism. You can actively practice a philosophy of selflessness and empathy for others. You can actively seek and destroy codependency in your own life. You can actively spend time focusing on your needs in a healthy and constructive way. You can build lasting interpersonal relationships based on unconditional love. By practicing a life of selflessness and fulfillment, you are healing emotional holes and scars.

As you move forward, letting go of hatred and resentment will become easier and easier. By changing your focus and removing your narcissistic parent from the center of your life, you have begun to blaze a new trail. Hatred and resentment will no longer be at the fore front of your experience. Hatred for your parent is unnecessary. You are enough on your own, and you have broken through the wounds inflicted by your parent's narcissism. You have stopped seeking to change your parent, and changed yourself instead.

You have left the past in the past to break the cycle of narcissism. This is an incredibly strong and powerful thing to have done. By forging a life free of narcissism, you are freeing yourself and others from its effects. You are ready to move into your future!

Conclusion

Congratulations! You have completed the book! You have worked at releasing your hatred, forming a stronger and more stable identity, and protecting the next generation. You are in the midst of forging an important, lifelong path full of joy. Remember that progress is continuous and can always be improved upon. Remember also that mistakes always happen, there will be bad days, and there will be difficulties ahead. Use this book as a resource and guide as you pave the way to your future. Come back to reassure yourself when you need it. If journaling has worked for you, continue to keep your journal as you move forward. Use this book as a baseline. The advice will always be here, ready and waiting as you encounter new situations. Remember that life is always changing. There will always be new people and new applications for the advice provided in this book!

Now that you have completed the book and are on a journey of self-love and discovery, it is still possible for you to maintain a relationship with your narcissistic parent, if you so desire. Especially if you have children, familial bonds are a vital resource. Your child may want to know their grandparent. Remember to continue re-using the advice in this book. Set your boundaries with your narcissistic parent, and do not allow these boundaries to be crossed. Do not become emotionally invested in your parent's expressions of love or approval. Always know that you are enough by yourself.

As you progress down your life path, continue practicing love, not dependency. Continue fostering love in all of your interpersonal relationships. Remember that love is the best cure for everything, and is the best way to release any feelings of hatred or resentment that may linger.

Your journey is just that: a journey. It will take time for you to continue taking back your life, and feelings of resentment and hatred may resurface, even after you may have believed them to be long gone. Stay the course! You are becoming a strong, accomplished, confident, loving individual, and you can relinquish the negative patterns in your life.

Thank you for purchasing this book. If you can, please leave a review! Let others know a little about your story, your goals, and your accomplishments.

Good luck to you in your journey!

Made in the USA
San Bernardino, CA
02 January 2019